Bear Bones
& Feathers

Also by Louise B. Halfe – Sky Dancer

awâsis – kinky and dishevelled
(Brick Books, 2021)

Burning in This Midnight Dream
(Brick Books, 2021; original edition Coteau Books, 2016)

The Crooked Good
(Kegedonce Press, 2021; original edition Coteau Books, 2007)

Blue Marrow
(Kegedonce, 2021; original edition Coteau Books, 2004)

Sôhkêyihta: The Poetry of Sky Dancer Louise Bernice Halfe
(Wilfred Laurier University Press, 2018)

Bear Bones
& Feathers

Louise B. Halfe – Sky Dancer

Brick Books

Library and Archives Canada Cataloguing in Publication

Title: Bear bones & feathers / Louise B. Halfe – Sky Dancer.
Other titles: Bear bones and feathers
Names: Halfe, Louise, 1953- author.
Description: Previously published: Regina, SK, Canada: Coteau Books, 1994.
Identifiers: Canadiana (print) 20210320419 | Canadiana (ebook) 20210326123 |
ISBN 9781771315784 (softcover) | ISBN 9781771315791 (HTML) | ISBN 9781771315807 (PDF)
Classification: LCC PS8565.A4335 B4 2022 | DDC C811/.54—dc23

We acknowledge the Canada Council for the Arts, the Government of Canada through the
Canada Book Fund, and the Ontario Arts Council for their support of our publishing program.

Cover painting by Vanessa Hyggen, *truth and reclamation.*
Author photo by Kimball V. Regier.
The book is set in Minion Pro.
Design by Marijke Friesen.
Printed and bound by Coach House Printing.

Original edition published by Coteau Books in 1994.
Edited by Patrick Lane.

Brick Books
487 King St. W.
Kingston, ON
K7L 2X7
www.brickbooks.ca

Though much of the work of Brick Books takes place on the ancestral lands of the Anishi-
naabeg, Haudenosaunee, Huron-Wendat, and Mississaugas of the Credit peoples, our editors,
authors, and readers from many backgrounds are situated from coast to coast to coast in
Canada on the traditional and unceded territories of over six hundred nations who have cared
for Turtle Island from time immemorial. While living and working on these lands, we are com-
mitted to hearing and returning the rightful imaginative space to the poetries, songs, and stories
that have been untold, under-told, wrongly told, and suppressed through colonization.

This book is dedicated to all residential school survivors,
to those who lost their lives, and to the generations
impacted by this history.

TABLE OF CONTENTS

FOREWORD TO THE NEW EDITION

My writing and ceremonial life began together. My people's history, culture, and spirituality infuse my poetics, while remaining universal to our shared human history.

The voices in *Bear Bones & Feathers* were lifted up in 1994. It has been in constant publication since, for which I thank my readers. Nevertheless, the more recent findings of the Truth and Reconciliation Commission, the National Inquiry into Missing and Murdered Indigenous Women and Girls, and the finding of many unmarked graves at Indian residential school sites have brought increased attention to the conflicted history we share. If anything, the work has even greater relevance now, twenty-eight years later.

May their voices continue to be heard from their "hallowed" ground and their stories ring in protest to their treatment while they lived.

The Truth and Reconciliation Commission "Calls to Action" provide a path for a renewed relationship. We must move beyond the emotional reaction to concrete change. It is my hope that *Bear Bones & Feathers* will contribute to the understanding, discussions, and change that we need, to create a better future for all our children.

All my relations.
Louise B. Halfe – Sky Dancer
January 2022

Bone Lodge

I sleep with *sihkos*.
In the fog she untangles
my braids.

I chant with robin
the shawl dance of
iskwêw.

I weave with spider
the journey's *ahcahk*.

I'm squirrel's mouth
the first time of pleasure.

I thunder *paskwâw-mostos*
in ribbons of sage.

I'm meat and bones,
dust and straw,
caterpillars and ants,
hummingbird and crow.

Of these I know
in the bones of the lodge.

Ghost Dance

I shall not be there. I shall rise and pass.
Bury my heart at Wounded Knee.
— Stephen Vincent Benet

They are in hills
in bush and prairie
clattering
shattered bones
chattering
laughing the dark.

Star after star
the wind carries the knuckle of
whistling songs.

They dance
gathering quills, moss,
clay, feathers, and
bear bones
to flesh themselves.

The drum beats
Big Foot
dancing
whistling eagles
laughing, laughing
these shattered,
gathered bones.

ayamihâwina — Old Rock Mother

There is no fear.
No reason to return.
I am gone
into the wilderness
of the sweat,
bleeding
Rock.

Crying for Voice

I must pull frog,
pry its webbed feet
from snails in
my throat.

Kneel, fold my hands,
invite weasel to untangle
my braids.

Boil duck, rabbit, fish,
scoop out brain,
eyes, and tongue,
roll them
inside my gut.

Pull out tapeworm,
chop onions, grind peppercorns,
fill the intestine
with fresh blood.

Boil bible and tripe,
clean off grass,
boil and boil
pebbles bubbling
soup.

Suck marrow from tiny bones,
fill the place
where frog left slime
and salted snails
fell.

I'm fluttering wind,
tobacco floating
against my face,
mosquitoes up my nostrils,
swatting memories
inside marrow.

Spirits

The veins throb
splattering
red the sky.

Comes the
night travelling
blood
swirling skirts
lifting
swishing moccasins.

Swaying bodies
in the beat of rawhide
in the beat of drum
the breathing Native lung.

Nodding heads
join swinging hands
shuffling deer-skinned feet
sweet bodies

babies
released from
the belly tie
spurt blood.

Cover hay and furred bed
wolf-mother rejoices
echoes the chant.

Red sky, night travelling
sweet bodies, four-legged ones
wolf-mother's blood
wolf-mother's voice.

Dancing, dancing the union
swirling skirts
moccasin feet.
The beating common lung.

pâhkahkos

Flying Skeleton
I used to wonder where
you kept yourself.
I'd hear you rattle about
scraping your bones

I opened a door
you grinned at me
your hollow mouth
stared through my heart
with empty eyes.

You lifted your bone hands
to greet me and I
ran without a tongue.

You jumped on my back
clinging to my neck you hugged
my mouth of flesh.

For a thousand years you were
the heavy bones
the companion who would not leave.

You knocked your skull
on my head
I felt your bone feet.
I dragged and dragged
I couldn't carry

your burden more.
I pried you loose
bone after bone.

We stood, skull to face
pâhkahkos, your many bones
exposed.
I, lighter than I could stand.

I fed you the drink of healing
you ran skeleton fingers
down your face and onto mine.

I gave you a prayer cloth
I wove a blanket of forgiveness
you covered us both, skeleton and flesh.

I gave you the smoke of truth
you lit your pipe to life
you lifted it to your ghostly mouth
to mine.

My *pâhkahkos* companion
my dancing Skeleton
my dancing friend.

We carry our bundles
side by side
bones and flesh.

nôhkom âtayôhkân 1

nôhkom âtayôhkân
a crown of sage
covers long strands of
fringed brome hair.

Ravines cut through
the soft leather
of your face.

Your mouth a
sensuous pink
wintergreen,
the movement of your long
strong neck
a graceful tree.

Old one with laughing eyes
wrap me in blanket grass
fragrant with sweet pine,
the woman-musk
of your rainfed forest.
Ground my wandering feet.

I want to cup
your breast,
a starving suckling child.
I want to drink the black and
white prayer beads
your milk spills.

nôhkom
there are no barren lands,
only a searching *ayisiyiniw*
snared in you.

nôhkom âtayôhkân 2

Your flaming flowers
spread on my breast,
your juices sticky between
my legs, my fingers.

I've watched life
blossom and fade from
your eyes.

You've folded flies
between your lips,
welcomed the swirl of
drinking hummingbirds.
You have coated bumblebees
with sunrays.

You have left me spent
lying open, dying
beneath the sun.

You, breathless,
sightless
beneath the snow.

Sundog Mate

Pregnant for so long
agonizing, dying
to birth.

The greased war
paint shone on the
sun's face,
sundogs laughing
a cheering squad
all my own.

Spread my legs
push, push,
caught bare-assed,
again.

Damn if I'm not ready
for the challenge,
the call
as I struggle.

Greasy make-up
smeared on the Sun's
sundog face,
laugh, cheer me on
sundog mate.

nôhkom, Medicine Bear

A shuffling brown bear
snorting and puffing
ambles up the stairs.

In her den
covered wall to wall
herbs hang ... carrot roots, yarrow,
camomile, rat-root,
and *câhcâmosikan*.

To the centre of the room she waddles,
sits with one leg out, the other hugged close.
She bends over her roots and leaves,
sniffs, snorts and tastes them
as she sorts them into piles.

She grinds the chosen few
on a small tire grater,
dust-devils settling into mole hills.
Her large brown paws take a patch
of soft deer skin
and wraps her poultice
until hundreds of tiny bundle-chains
swing from the rafters.

The brown labouring bear
nôhkom, the medicine woman,
alone in her attic den
smoking slim cigarettes
wears the perfume of sage, sweetgrass,
and earth medicine ties.

nôhkom, the medicine bear,
healer of troubled spirits.
A red kerchief on her head,
blonde-white braids hang below her breasts.
She hums her medicine songs
shuffling alone in her den where
no light penetrates, no secrets escape.

She bends and her skirt drapes
over her aged beaded moccasins.
She brushes the potions off her apron.
A long day's work complete,
nôhkom ambles down the stairs,
sweeps her long skirt behind her,
drapes her paws on the stair rails,
leaves her dark den and its medicine powers
to work in silence.

Off with Their Heads

nôhkom
used to take the
visiting tomcats
and ever so gently
wrap a snare wire
around their necks.

From the clothesline
we'd watch the cats
kicking, scratching,
clawing

until

they hung

limp.

Later
I'd go and examine
the stiffs.

Their lifeless eyes,
blood-filled like
late summer rosehips,
the foam around their
mouth land-salt
on a dry lake.

Flies swarmed
around the dried shit.
Ground beetles
ate their meal.

Cat stench
filled my nostrils.
I'd stumble away
clawing the invisible snare
for fresh air.

nôhkom would sit at the window
with a cup of tea,
puffing her pipe,
staring at the tomcats.

nôhkom's Ice Cream and Syrup

She'd sit on her bed
a huge broody hen
rolling long slim cigarettes
grinning through smoke-stained teeth.

"*nôhkom*," I'd say, "Ice cream and syrup."
"*hâw, kiskiman, asam picikîskisîs*," she'd say.

And *kiskiman*, my cousin, a miniature *nôhkom*,
would scuttle about, a cockroach
setting the table.

An enamel pot of woodstove tea,
a roasted rabbit, head and all,
legs poking out, bannock
and melted tallow: dinner is served.

"*nôhkom*, ice cream and syrup."
She'd crack the rabbit head open
hand me a spoon and I'd scoop and eat
the ice cream dish.

In a chipped stone saucer
she'd pour muskeg tea,
stir in *âmow-mêyi* and
I'd slop slabs of bannock in my syrup treat.

nôhkom would watch,
clucking her pleasure.
Smoking her long, un-cut, hand-rolled cigarettes.
She'd hand me a peppermint,
smooth her wrinkled apron,
with a wave she'd dismiss
kiskiman and me.

Behind her back *kiskiman* would pinch,
determined he was *nôhkom's* favorite,
and I'd shove and punch,
pleased that *kiskiman*, again, had to wait on me.

She Told Me

She always told me
to take a willow branch
and gently whip the spirits
out of the house
calling, calling

âstam we are leaving
âstam do not stay.

She always told me
to put the food away at night
to cover the dishes
or the spirits
would crackle and dance
whistle in our ears
and drive us mad.

I obeyed.

She always told me
never to eat the guts of
animals while I was pregnant
or the baby would be born
with a rope around the neck.

I yearned for the guts.

She always told me
that *nôhkom,* the medicine bag,
had given her three cigarettes.
That's why the lizards
walked around inside her head.

I watched the flicker of her tongue.

She always told me
never to walk over men
while I was in my moon
or they would die from my power.

I thought that was the idea.

Grandma's Apprentice

In the end she petrified me.

Her braids, snakes over each breast.
A constant stream of tobacco juice ran down her chin.
She never spoke a word of English except to laugh
"fuck you" through thin closed lips.

She was Grandma's apprentice. And when Grandma died
she took over the dark long into the night
under the light of a coal oil lamp.
The smell of skunk crept under the door and woke me,
her grunting and spitting in the tobacco can,
the grinding and pounding of roots never ceased
till *mihkwâskikan* sang the first song.

She told me, "Never go alone to the spring well
down by the creek,
Grandma lives in that water."
Yet
she'd pour crystal cold water in the dipper and slurp
knowing all the while the water was spirit. In the end
her fingers curled, frozen claws,
her eyes black peering from under the leaves of lids.
Her mouth a sliver.
Her back gnarled as short prairie aspen,
roots digging dry sand.

I offered her the spring well on her deathbed.
She looked into the deeps of the glass.
It was only she who saw the cloudy white mist
that settled into her eyes
as she parted her cracked lips and rasped,
"*kinêpik*" and sighed.

Men in My Life

nimosôm

I never knew him. He was the man with blue/green eyes. His white/blond hair cropped close to his skin. I'd watch him standing in the yard with a smoke in his hand quiet as the land. His beloved Sport stood beside him, tail wagging. I remember *nimosôm* best with his Clyde horses, the leather in his hand, the firm gentle giddy-up. And when he wasn't in the field plowing or strolling the woods with the .22, he was beside *nôhkom* serving her sweatlodge with hot rocks or lying beside her watching through a haze of smoke. My father tells me *nimosôm's* Indian name was *apisc-âhkiskôs*, or The Prairie Walker. I used to think that meant He Who Took Little Steps, but it is old, pure Cree. The Walker is a Prairie bird, just like *nimosôm*.

I woke with the song and dance of robins, sweetgrass smells from my father's bedroom but it was the cigarette smoke drifting in from the outside that prompted me to step quietly out of bed. And there on the lawn chair my father sat. He didn't look like *nimosôm*. My father was taller than the pine tree in my childhood memory. He walked with the land on his back and a cane to hold his spirit. His face was grey, his cheeks caved. His head shone in the sun with whispers of silver, hands sun-stained. He sat quietly, facing the sun. He told me he too was The Walker.

My husband is slouched over the soil, he lets the damp darkness loose through thick fingers. He straightens and brushes his face, hair tumbling around blue/green eyes, the sun catching the horse sandy coloring of his hair. His hands are large, firm and gentle, patient in planting seedlings. In the woods he offers tobacco. A rifle stands beside him. He hunts sparingly, walking the footsteps of my father's dream, sharing the footsteps of *nimosôm's* vision.

He Has Gone to Ground

Sometimes he wears skunk bone
or tailfeather earrings,
dyed horsehair wrapped around wire
weaved through his hair.
He bathes in sage or cedar,
sweating through breathing rocks.

When the leaves are laughing, fresh from birth,
he builds a lodge into the hill.
Like some young gopher he sweeps dirt over his shoulder,
sweat and blood running hot.

Bug-eyed spitting grasshoppers,
mink-furred caterpillars,
black ants pulling dead flies,
spiders in gunny sacks,
sparrows, hawks are his visitors.
He hears only the heart.

In sleep he sees rocks with big feet.
Old women sitting at the earth altar.
Old man smoking pipe.
A demon covered in silk,
a small woman with a whip.
He takes flight riding horses through forest,
lakes and distant lands.

Dreams, he dreams and dreams and dreams.

His lips want breast milk,
the marsh wetness of woman.
His stomach wants rubber cinnamon candies,
sweet raspberries and wild rice.
He is a mud-hen
swimming in black earth,
feet scratching his leg,
digging holes with his toes.

When the chickadees sing
he will rise,
watch the fading moon,
watch the sun-dance.
Raise his pipe and
sing the prayers of his death.
He will walk his dreams.

Rituals

The black-haired woman is tucked in her rabbit
skin blanket. Water trickles down her face.

The white-haired woman takes the grease-stained
red kerchief from her head and carefully wraps the
gartersnake skin, paper thin.
Earth smells weave around the room.
She anoints the waiting woman with
deer grease and places the crown
around the still black head.

A man with snow hair
sits puffing a cigarette,
smoke haloed.
Green eyes pierce through eyelid slivers.

The white-haired woman turns the black head.
The razor makes little slits on her temples.
Blood sweats.
Withered lips hover
over a hollow buffalo horn and suck.
Her tongue flickers
on a cigarette paper as she pastes peppered roots
against the moist flesh.

The black-haired woman moans while the withered
lips flap. She's a blown-out tire
on a gravel road, scolding.

Elder's Waltz

nôhkom and *nimosôm*
are going dancing.

Tobacco offerings
ribbon cloths
Elder's murmuring
prayer songs.

nôhkom wears pony beads
flowing flowered dress
a wide beaded belt with
hanging silver trinkets.

Campfires
muskeg tea boiling
smoke
meat drying.

nôhkom and *nimosôm*
are going dancing.

nôhkom has been working for hours
on her deer-skin moccasins
soaked in tea
kneaded and stretched
dried like flannel.
nôhkom lifts leathered legs

tugs and pulls
wraps and wraps the
hightop flaps and
rawhide thongs.

Chokecherry leather
pemmican pouch
kinnikinnick green
briar pipe.

Her long blonde-white braids
greased with bear fat
gloss as if she's spent
hours with her porcupine brush.

nimosôm
cropped blond-white hair
slicked down too with bear fat.
He slips on buckskin quilled jacket
over his velvet tanned leggings.
Beads and beads sparkle from
moccasin feet.

People laughing
skynight
sparkling
with fire embers.

He searches for the white-skinned drum.
His footsteps shuffle dance
to music in his head.
Tonight, tonight
the departed spirits
will feast on the bone's marrow.

nôhkom and *nimosôm*
are going dancing.

People squat
hands touch
circle forming.

The white-skinned drum
sends its musical tongue
colouring the air.

Blueberry, sweetgrass
offering and burning.

nôhkom and *nimosôm*
are dancing.

Grouse

I placed his hand on the paper,
a grouse's fantail
splayed on a dancing tree.
My drawing stick outlines
as he patiently waits.

I purr into his jackrabbit ears
and nibble his lobes.
The braided candle
flames our shadows
against the mud-straw walls.

We've few evenings like this
my father and I
when his voice drums
hunting stories.
His eyes spirit dance,
and his hands wave,
curve and buck
into creatures of the night.

Tonight I've captured them.
They rest
bark on cool leaves
and warm against my cheek.

Wagon Ride

I lean on the wagon boards
and squint over the horse's head.
Blankets of firefly snow sparkle.

Horse's nostrils
bellow clouds and form
halos around their bending heads.

Their broad bodies move
slowly through unbroken trail.

Swishing tails
they fart
as fresh horse manure
fills the air.

I look back and view
the glazing broken path
as fresh snow covers
tracks.

I peer at the skies,
stick out my tongue
catch tiny diamonds,
cross my eyes to look at
the snowflakes before they
melt on the tip of my nose.

I peep at Papa.
He's dressed in his trapping beaver mitts
and fraying hudson's bay coat.
A winchester stands by his side.
His head is tilted. He's listening to
the crackling trees.
Tiny antler icicles hang from his eyelids
and underneath his nose.
His cheeks are apple red.
Still
he puffs on his hand-rolled du maurier.

Today there is no smashing fist
and kicking working boots,
no thunder of an outraged bull,
no snarling of a rabid cat

Just me and Papa
cold-bound by the mute,
freezing wind.

Chokecherries

She has ghosts of blueberry shiners
and an arm glazed in strawberry stains.
Her foot is still walking sideways.
Now she stands
in front of his bed.

Her voice doesn't waver.
"*awâsisak* they love you and look after you
I don't understand why."
She points to her foot.
She tells him, "The lizard hasn't stopped
and I still walk the dark."

He'd drink moose milk,
beat phantom lovers he caught in her arms
rocks held in the ball of his fist,
and when his fever was spent
he'd be back in the woods axing trees,
snaring rabbits or stalking deer.

She whispers, "I will stop the
tongue of lizard. Maybe
the winter squall in my chest will die."
He lies with staples in his gut,
chokecherries on his breath
and the slough in his eye.

Loving Obscenities

She always wore
those stupid
indian affairs glasses
that looked like
the slanted eyes of
a Siamese cat.

He always walked
stooped
puffing on export a,
disguising his whisky breath
with spearmint gum.

She always wore
a black and blue shiner
every Friday and Saturday night.
Those stupid fist marks
of his drama attacks.

His eyes moved swiftly,
examining every visible track,
poking and stubbing his feet
at the sign of suspected
visiting lovers.

And
when they were together,
Mother and Father,
he would walk ahead
muttering his loving obscenities
while she walked softly behind
staring through his head
with those cheap
indian affairs glasses.

Body Politics

Mama said,

Real woman
don't steal
from the sky and wear clouds
on their eyelids.

Real woman
eat rabbit well-done
not left half-raw
on their mouth.

Real woman
have lots of meat
on their bones.
They're not starving,
hobbled horses
with bony, grinding hips.

Real woman caress
with featherstone hands
not with falcon fingernails
that have never worked.

When she was finished talking
she clicked her teeth,
lifted her arse,
and farted
at the passing
city women.

Lizard's Curse

She came in the form of a slippery lizard
with a feather in her mouth.

She wrapped her shiny flesh
over my woman's hills and crawled my crevice.

My eyes puffed and swelled
hailstones on my face.

My head ached
heavy with rocks.

I sought the healing
mountain
and the ocean's salt.

The soft pounding
of a beating drum
and a woman's chanting song.

The sweet scent of cedar
drifted in the wind

pulling, pulling
the power of the lizard.

The skin stretched,
and my wintering flesh
hung loose against my bones.

The lizard's claws and tattered feather
left its trail of scratches in my womb.

Bled dry of tears,
I let the ocean's coolness
flush my wound.

The mountain cedar released healing sap,
its sacred smoke smudged my temples.
The throb of darkness slipped

with the last shedding of the lizard's curse
and the woman's chant.

Free from Grandma

By the bonfire
she sits
just like Grandma
with one leg tucked,
the other straight out.

As she chats
she rolls
the bannock dough
on the willow stick
and props it near
the hot coals.

She pokes and strokes
one smouldering coal
and lets the ember
die beside her.

The bannock stick
turns brown and
she turns it slowly
to let the other
side bake.

With the dead
charcoal
she outlines the bottom
of her eyelids explaining
the twitching is

driving her mad
and must be cared for
because warnings are dark.

The bonfire dances
as she adds more wood,
adjusting the raw meat
that hangs on the tripod.

In the hot sun
she sits
with blackened eyes,
glasses perched at the
bottom of her nose,

flipping through
True Romance.

She eyes
the bannock,
eyes
the fire.
Waving the smoke,
hunched over like Grandma.

Tuberculosis Thief

Playing
on the aspen floors by
Grandma's hearth, memories
drifted of her mama's warmth.

Listening to
the talking box
she heard her mama's voice.

She probed the nylon mesh,
poked and shook the voice box
calling Mama, Mama.
pê-kîwê, pê-kîwê.

Hands gripped on the knobs of
the lying box,
she bowed her curly head while
the talking spirits drifted
and took her mama away.

Grandma's hand stroked her
soaking cheeks while
the child of sapling height
thought her mama dead.
The tuberculosis thief
hid in her mama's lungs
and buried her
three years
behind the sanatorium walls.

Womanchild

Your calloused burnt hands
smoothed the snarewire and formed a loop.
You said, it's so the rabbit won't get
loose and die a useless death.
Each dawn before the raven called
you nudged me awake and shooed me out the door
to see what we snared in the dark.
I walked proudly home with what we caught.
You peeled the skin, chopped off the balls,
flipped them on the woodstove, and fed me
the delicate taste.

Go and chop some
wood, you say.
I'll bake you
jelly rolls and cinnamon bread.
I saw and chop, toss and haul
till the wood is stacked to the cabin wall.
Tired, I lie on your bed.
Your gentle hands cover me with our crazy-quilt.
I dream of nutmeg and cinnamon cloves
and wake to the hissing of the lamp.

Dragging blankets through the woods,
you asked me not to breathe,
not to whimper, not to cry.
He's drunk again, you whispered,
as you made me a bed of spruce boughs.

There you sat while the moonlight walked
and the night hawk whistled by.

You handed me that long thick needle
with bright yellow yarn.
On the floor I crawled
behind you proudly sewing footsize stitches
on your jig-saw quilt.
I heard you crooning
what a hard-working wife I'd make.

Your swollen knees speak of crawling.
Your toothless mouth gums the Safeway rabbit.
Your arthritic hands ache to bake.
Your pleurisy mocks your laughter
beside that man wrapped inside your crazy quilt.
You the womanchild, my mother of wrinkled winters.

Ukrainian Hour

She spins from her belly
button-lint weaving,
pulls from her mouth
finger-stump stories.
She knits horsehair,
whipping the stick
of laughing songs.

She weaves on her knees,
humming rabbit fur stitched
between sheets of rags,
the land filled with
picket fences and tumbleweeds.

When the coal-oil lamp dances
and the cabin fire is still
wîsahkêcâhk jigs the two step
on Ukrainian Hour,
swirling her skirt,
whirling her children
in the safety of night.

Aborting

I remember
the braided wick's
tiny flame
smoking our shadows

Mama lying in bed

the children
the dirt floor
making roads
and wooden squares.

Mama getting up

falling

the children's
screams and screams
trying to lift Mama.

The fire is out.
Build the fire, she said.

　　　That's all
　　　I remember.

Fog Inside Mama

I'm going to take you home, Mama.

Yes, to that log shack where Papa skinned beaver
on the dirt floor.

The grass is tall. There'll be lots of mosquitoes.

Yes, Mama, the old fridge is still there and no, there's no
lightning going through to make it breathe.

The windows are broken and the barn swallows have built
their nest where the stovepipe used to smoke.

Oh Mama don't, Papa hasn't walked on that land, not for
years. Not since the last time he crushed your ribs on that
fridge.

He's on skid row somewhere.

It's safe. All we have are the old ghosts drifting
through the clouds of our heads.

Yes, Mama. I remember the tadpoles from the slough swishing
inside my red fireman's boots. They were my favorite boots.
I slept in them, I never took them off till those little
swimming snakes squished inside.

Your bones are tired and I can't find the road. I've got a
fly in my eye and it's making the rain fall from my nose.

Yes, I remember the lard pail hanging from my stomach
with a belt of twine. I'd pick so fast trying to beat Papa,
the berries drummed. Only
I never won. Papa, he picked twigs and bugs and insisted that
he had won the race.

What was that Mama?

Oh yeah, for school I had your bannock and fried rabbit.
I'd eat it *kîmôc* in the bathroom so the white kids
wouldn't laugh at me. Oh, it was good. So good.

You want some tea and a cigarette?

Yes, we're almost there.

I can see the old shack, the outhouse, the chicken coop,
the jalopy.

Yes, Mama we're going home. No more hiding.

First Moon

I
squat
in the curve of the lodge.
The air filled with muskeg and sweet blood
in dried cakes.

I cup the warmth
between my legs.
My fingers stick.
The blood ribbon
is velvet,
violent against
my flesh.

Moon rolled in my tongue,
around my fingers, and
in my bones.

I squeeze my legs,
tight.
I flow anyway, I flow.
I poke, I plug.
My finger is an infant rabbit
slaughtered out of the mother's belly.

Will my baby be a rabbit?
Wet, slippery, and red
like the silent creek between my legs?

I sit in my lodge
tangle of legs and arms.
Clumps of wet moss on the skin of earth,
mats between my legs.
The moon's child
bleeding the night.

Emma

Emma had scabs
all over,
under her beehive hair,
under her panties,
everybody
shunned her.

She hid from the sun.
If she didn't
the hot rays would get her
scratching
until
rivers of red glistened
and
clusters of dried meat covered her.

I played with Emma.
We formed a leper colony.

Shunned,
we had our moon together.
Nobody ever knew.

Emma she walked straight and proud
with that rag between her legs
I walked with a book in front of me.

Scabs and rags, Emma and me.

Bareback in the Snakehills

She went home with
cowboy legs
unable to close them.

Her grandma said some boys
had shoved
their *micakisîs*
up her
hole.

She doesn't know where
Grandma got that idea.

The doctor said it was a
broken
hymen.

She didn't know that
hymns were sung between
her legs.

Just blood on rags
that ran
from bareback riding
in the hills.

Maintain the Right

Sixteen,
wearing white shorts
platform shoes.

He picked her up,
drove
down a country road.

Stopped and pushed her out.
Ordered a *blow job*.
She didn't understand.

He pushed her head
between his legs.

Said a girl dressed like her
gave head
to cops like him.

Her hair held by
gripping hands,
her mouth full.

She gagged
with every motion.

Mud stained,
she walked back to
the cruise car

and shoved her fingers
down her throat.

He
watched.

Ditch Bitch

She never felt the piss of dogs
bleeding in the rain,
tongues of thistle weeds
tearing her moonlit mud skin.

She lay in this ditch
a ghost of twenty-three earths.

A woman older than the trees
of the Drumheller coulees
carrying a knapsack of roots,
pushing beer bottles
into the large folded apron
of her skirt,
singing the morning song

waniskâ
pê-wâpan ôma
âsay piyêsîsak
nikamowak
miyohtâkwan
kitaskînaw.

The song stirred the ghost
and her outstretched arm
fell on the chest of the mother.

Men plastered to her mouth,
her belly and her spoon,
stripped her skin,
fell to the wasted water of blood.

The ditch,
an open mouth of mudslides,
formed a lodge of sticks and hides.
The old woman held a horse blanket,
covered the holes of the hurting flesh.

Together they sang,
drumming the song

Arise
dawn has come
already the birds sing
and the earth
delights with life.

Valentine Dialogue

I got bit.

By what?

A snake bite.

Where?

In my spoon. Gon er eeah.

Wholee sheeit.

Love he dold me.

I have a pain in my heart.

Fuckin liar.

Hate all of them.
Dink day can hang dair
balls all over da place.

Cross my legs next dime.

Mudder says day all alike.

Snake in dair mouth,
snake in dair pants.
Guess dat's a forked dongue.

Mudder says I'll never lift it down.
Fadder says I'm nothin but a cheap dramp.

Da pain in my heart hurts, hurts.

My brown dits,
day shame me.
My brown spoon
fails me.

Dired of sinning.
Dew ya dink confession will help?
Dew ya dink prayers will clean me?
Maybe I be born again.
Da pain in my heart hurts, hurts.

Durty priest
jest wants da durty story.

Fuckin men.

Day dink I a cheap badge
to hang on dair sleeve, as if
I an easy spoon.

A dongue in dair mouth.
A dongue in dair pants.
No nothin 'bout the heart.
No nothing 'bout my soul.

Day lookit my mouth.
Must be a nice mouth
cuz I see da look
in dair eyes.

And my mouth
wants
to feel dair wet lips.

It's Mudder's fault,
never told me right from wrong.
Fadder's fault,
always say Mudder a slut.
Guess I must be one too.
Guess I showed dem.

Meet nice man one day.
Maybe brown.
Maybe white.
Maybe black.
Maybe yellow.

Won't show
my body dalks.
Won't dell
'bout da snake bite.

Eatin' Critters

We would stand
on the skirt of the hill,
survey the stubble land
as hawk eyes marked our kill.

Ears like wings on a gliding hawk,
ball cap low on his brow,
lard pail and killing rock,
chewing gum with me in tow.

I'd wet my finger
to test the wind.
He'd scold me if I slowed
and pinch my suntanned skin.

Tilted head and twitching ears
would listen to the gopher's pierce.
We'd spot our ground-belly meal,
race to the ditch and fill the pail
and give the hole a chug-a-lug.
When the whiskers breathe,
catch the gopher's tail.

Flatten his head with my rock
throw his dripping skin in the pail
swagger my hips like a satisfied cock
clowning home with my brother's grin.

Sugar Beat

Lethbridge
         Taber
               Raymond
                     Coaldale

Day all da same.
Busting my ass
hoeing down dem weeds
'tween sugar beets.

Eight quarters a hour
for a friggin' sun burn.
Me durns dar black.
Muskkills aches.

Drag dired body to
chicken coop hut.

Fly Indian steak
stir a bit o'
mac a roonie.

Count da bed bugs
crawling der way to
stinking mattress.

Itch and scratch
before I hit da pillow
friggin' chickens
left der mess
in sugar shack.

Domorrow paycheque
buy a beer, buy players,
catch a movie, pretend I
still a kid.
Eat bobcorn
and watch
Kemo Sabe
Lone Ranger.

i bring my sins to geezuz

dear geezuz

i liked it when my mouth stayed
stucked on his
i never wanted
to take them off
years later
i feel his wetness

riding that greyhound
sitting in the back seat
his little brother asleep
i feel his hard

we played cowboys and indians
chasing each other
no one else exist
one fleeting kiss
was all i got

when my tits exploded
he ignored me
i lurked beside the girls
he fingered

one drunken night he came
and slept
six feet deep
he buried
my dream.

nîcimos

1960
William walked by my desk
and dropped a torn crumpled paper.
Teacher is not looking.
Hiding behind a book
I carefully reveal the scribbled
words.

William is tall with silky brown skin,
his gleaming black eyes
look over at me while I hide behind my book,
one eye peering out at him.

1966
I ran into Marvin on the staircase.
I mumble a shy hi and dared to look at him
as he walked up.
He looked down and stopped my flight by the
whisper of my name
and cupped my chin as he leaned over the rail
to plant a soft kiss.
For months I touched my mouth, Marvin still
hovering over me.

Marvin and I use to play cowboys and Indians.
Him in his halfbreed green eyes, mother said
he was treaty, would run after me with two guns blazing
and I the Indian would slow my running feet
so Marvin could kill me and I'd fall.

1968
I was in grade 8 when William stroked my jeans
and his hands slid over my training bra.
My body tingled and I shot out of the cabin, crimson
on my face. I never saw William again,
they say he married and became an alcoholic.

1973
Smoking grass high in the stone hills
emerald eyes and moustache smile
charmed the clothes off my skin.

1975
Sixty dollars I paid for his wedding band,
fifty dollars he paid for mine.
The elopement in some penthouse,
the dinner party at Prince Edward Hotel
of Edmonton lobster and prime Alberta steak.

Valentine's day he gave me daffodils with
two babies on my breast.

And I
in turn
gave him tangerine, plum, candy apple lips.

Thieves

Daddy lifts
his fists
knocks it against
Mommy's cheek.

Brother tells me
I can't pee standing up.

Daddy he praises me
when I chop wood
and bring rabbits home
and hoe down weeds.

.

In mission school
the nuns cut my long hair
cover me
in thick dresses.

When I shower
they cover my tits and my bum
take a scrub brush to my back.

That boy he corners me
touches
my spoon and makes
me cry.

In church on my knees
I pray to father
about that dirty hole.

In the classroom
when I talk
when I write about the boosh
they laugh and scold me
make me stand in the corner.

And that girl
with thick lips
mean talk
her stick
scares me.

And that nun
in black robes
with prayer beads
makes me peel potatoes
makes me iron sheets
makes me polish the floors
and strips my lumpy bed.

•

I feel good with beer
drink the boys
wear make-up
sexy clothes
show off my legs.

I travel to Jamaica
go to university
laugh at that old
broken English.

I've dumped religion
sit cross-legged in the
sweatlodge, chanting songs.

I've married   *well.*

Boarding School

In the late fall
ice waited
outside our cabin.

Inside
crackling fire
licked the guts
of the woodstove.
The coal oil lamp
flickered in the
one-room shack.

Two white-skins
talked in tongues.
Father's long face
stretched further
to the floor.
Mother's crimson cheeks
turned like swirling ashes
in the stovepipe.

Behind
Mother's draping dress
a six-year-old sister.
Her small fist
white against
brown skin.

I sat behind a
thick home-made
wooden table,
trembling.
My stomach couldn't hold
the fresh cinnamon roll.

The air was
wrapped in
raven darkness.

namôya mâskôc.
It's a mistake.
Father's voice
shook.
Mother swayed.

The white-skins
left.
The cold seeped in the
cracks of the door,
its fingers wrapped
in silence.

The world
was silent.

The family gone.

The family not ever more.

The Residential School Bus

A yellow caterpillar,
it swallows them up.

The little brown ones their stained
faces in the windows   skinny and thick
black braids   pressing hands
grease the glass.

On its back the caterpillar
carries hand-sewn canvas bags.

Outside against the evening sun
the mothers, the fathers,
shrink.

They cannot look
at the
yellow caterpillar.

•

The building is huge
with long white empty hallways.

A child walks softly
the echo runs ahead of her.

The smell of lysol
and floor wax
overwhelms the memory of wood smoke
and dirt floors.

•

At night the little ones
press their bodies
between cold starched sheets.
Somewhere
someone
in the huge dorm
sobs quietly.

The child
clenches
two purple
suckers
underneath her pillow.

She won't eat them,
not for a
while.

•

They line up for breakfast
and receive wonderful bowls of porridge.

She loves porridge.
Her mama always made her porridge.

She looks up and sees
her favourite brother.

Ivan's ears look like
two gliding hawks.
They've given him a crew cut.

Charlie the eldest brother
is in the big boys' room.
She doesn't see him
and doesn't care.

Her eyes linger on
Ivan. They smile.

She swallows
the porridge
that is stuck in her
throat.

•

Geezuz
is always mad.

She sits too often
in the confessional.
She kneels too often
in front of geezuz.

•

The vision box
collects people
and makes them dance.

She turns the buttons
and the dancing people
turn into black and white lines.

She kneels
in the corner.

The girl
with the mean stick
and fat mouth
hovers near her.
She's a
huge night moth
beating her wings
against the dance.

•

They've arrived.
Wagonloads of
mothers, of fathers.

The children have been
berry picking.

Sister Treebow
is like that girl
with the big lips.

Sister's lips stick out
further. The arrival of
mothers, of fathers
makes her madder.

The children
stand around the corner
of the building
wondering whose
mother, whose father
was there.

She didn't want to hope.

Father Brown
in his long black dress
calls out names.

Times are scheduled.

In the bare parlour
they sit,
Mother, Father, Ivan,
and her big brother.

Their stiff hugs,
she wants more
but can't.

The stiffness stays.

The glass between the parlour
and the hallway is marked
with grease-stained hands
and smudges of
rain.

•

The yellow school bus
waits.

Ships on the Reserve

I grew up in mud
my dolls earth
scratchings
on lye-painted walls
straw   horsehair
a bluebird's nest
plastered by my fingers
between wind whistling
aspen cracks and
mother's quilts.

I never saw a TV
never heard of ships
yet
ships were in the
bowels of the earth
where I dug tunnels
and ate earth crumbles
devilled with tiny red
and white eggs
I'd stuff till my
tongue thickened
in blackness.

I'd emerge
slap bannock dough
on slabs of cardboard
charcoal stick figures
with long eyelashes

massive hearts
smiles stretched
across the slough
where string snakes sang.

My ship moved and
I travelled in brick walls
starched, clean as Mary
in her bluebird robe
heart throbbing
plastered against her
chest. I pried it loose
saw through the smile.

My ship, my ship
mud   bricks
crumbling in my mouth.

nitôtêm

He was tired of having his ears pulled,
squeezed, and slapped
by sister superior. They bled and
swelled, scabbed and scaled like the brick wall.
Often he didn't hear the sister shouting
and clapping her orders at him
or the rest of the little boys.
The others, when they could,
would nudge him so he could lip-read sister's words.

He was embarrassed to undress in front of all the boys
and especially sister.
At home he always looked out the window
when someone was undressing. Here everyone looked
and laughed at your private parts.
Soon they too were no longer private.

He suffered in silence
in the dark. A hand muffled his mouth
while the other snaked his wiener. He had no
other name, knew no other word. Soon it was no
longer just the hand but the push, just a gentle
push at first, pushing, pushing. Inside the
blanket he sweated and felt the wings
of pleasure, inside his chest the breath burst
pain, pleasure, shame. Shame.

•

On the reserve he had already raped two
women, the numbers didn't matter.
Sister superior was being punished. It was
father who said it was woman's fault
and that he would go to hell.

He walked, shoulders slightly stooped
and never looked directly at anyone.
When spoken to he mumbled into his chest.
His black hair covered his eyes. He no longer
tried to lip-read, no longer studied the
brick wall.

Bruises Are Part of Daddy's Job

His arms lie
heavy across my stomach.
He snores, dreams of
frozen fish.

The telephone rings and rings
his arm flails in the dark.

He snores
nightmares of
battered women, death rattles,
bar fights.

He slams the phantom phone.

The hospital gown flaps
he's a pelican in the emergency room
feet stuffed in two
different shoes.

My son crawls into the grooved
folds of crumpled sheets. His face
a trail of sleep, and shadows on
his lips. I rock him, whisper

bruises are part of Daddy's job
gassing, mending, patching. Shhh.

Tribal Warfare

She pressed her tits
hard into his mouth, against his chest
held his balls in her fist.

He was so drunk he couldn't get it up.
He had promised her a good one,
damn good.

She was so horny she
cried between his legs.

Later
in the psychiatric ward
the doctor asked why
she took so many pills.

She couldn't tell him
how she wanted it so bad, it shamed her.
She couldn't tell him
the foreigner slept many nights
spent, while she wept
for *nêhiyawak.*

Hoop Dancer

She was told take a mirror and
look at your spoon when
she talked about
how

she square-danced
in a half-breed dress
white husband in her arms.

How

she sat in the bleachers
wrapped in a blanket
wind blowing feathers
humming powwow songs.

How

she watched her husband blow
the eagle whistle
his shoulders, his knees
bobbing
blue eyes fixed on the
Sundance Tree.

How

she whistled, and hooted
stamping her feet
betting nickels and quarters
at the rodeo grounds.

And how

she's on the cruise ship
wearing a four hundred dollar
gown, lips painted red
staining the sky.

She talked
softly of being
crushed through to the bone
and willed the heart to pound.

Tonight when the music stops
and her son's footsteps sleep
she will close the bathroom door
press the mirror between her legs
as pipe tobacco fills
her space of song.

stones

men
day hang dere balls
all over da place.

what I didn't no
is day
whack dem
fundle dem
squeeze dem
dalk to dem
whisper to dem
scream at dem
beg dem
pray to dem
g ah sh
even
swear at dem.

I no dese
cuz I followed dem
at dat place
where day use ghost berries
nd buff alow sticks
nd play in da
buff a low mud
nd day use dat
stick
nd whack dem
berries

into
dem
gopher holes.

dere all ways drying
to put dem
dere balls everywhere
why
I evin saw dem
at dem dere
dinner dables
coloured balls
wit a big long broom
boking,
rolling,
nd smacking dem
all together
into
six holes
in dat dable.

g ah sh
wit all dat whacking
day shood of come
a long dime ago
nd be satisfied.

but no
dere still
jiggling dem
between dere legs

drying to find
different hole
to put dem in.

dem balls by now
should be so heavee
day make dere walk
hard
liddle bit
like dem
African elephants
I saw on
DV.

Hamilton's Graveyard

A seed was planted in the North Bay rain, cries, sweet cries
of night birds nesting in sheets of damp leaves.

The seed grew and swelled in the buried bodies of
my guts.

I wanted refund for my ten-dollar IUD. Slanted
my eyes at the touch of the physician's hand. Swore
at the man whose pleasure I carried.

At home I thought of my mother's bitter root that would shred
my growing womb. I heard the voice of the sweetgrass braids.
I thought of another baby twisted like a knotted tree, her head
an empty bowl. My hand rested on my swollen belly.

It started with liver sliding into the toilet. Later IV
vodka to still the belt around my waist. Then an incision
traced the equator across my skin and delivered
her into my frozen arms.

She died with a head of wet dark hair shining in the butter
dish. The rain fell down my drying breasts.

Gifts for the Child

He thought of
spawning fish,
chickadees and ravens
soaring the sky
when he came inside her.

She thought of
darning socks, knitting and quilting,
pounding chokecherries, rendering fat
for pemmican winter feasts
while the aspen juice ran.

The child arrived squealing
between her legs,
an infant rabbit in elder's skin,
chokecherry stain on her back.
He smeared brain of chickadee
on the roof of the child's mouth and
she fed her marrow fat.

Rainbow Babies

They travelled west across the prairies
to visit the site of a sixty-seven
year old burial. Infant bones that
long left their song beyond the trees.
They live two hours away from
my daughter's grave. A place where dozens
of babies keep their wings warm, rubbing
bones together, dancing fireflies over
the lake, lighting candles in plastic
bouquets.

My husband and I offer saskatoons, deer
meat and wild rice to the one who
breathes the wind, the one joined
in laughter with her burial companions.
The one whose fingers I did not reach. I
will carry a bouquet of wheat, string their
heads in song. Leave it for the old bones,
the living bones, and for the wind.

Snake

I am a snake.

Comfortable in my skin.
Too comfortable. Became fat.
Cannot see. Peering
from under these hooded eyes.
Cannot hear. Skin has grown
over my ears. Cannot smell to test the air.
Thought this staleness was normal.

I am a snake.

Cheeks puffed.
Thought I could see everywhere.
Didn't realize I hadn't scaled the wall.
Didn't realize my belly was all I scratched.
Sleeping inside my skin.

I am a snake.

I begin to crack.
Shed the old. Slowly peel.
My new head emerges.
Tongue tastes the wind. Caution fills my
every bone. Raw my skin is.

I am a snake.

Vulnerable above and below. Hot rock,
cold rock. Slithering off, slithering in, slithering
down, up, around, away.

I am a snake.

Equivocating tongue.
I see the light. I see the dark.

Hold Me Tight

I went inside his belly.
I found magpies feeding on maggots,
berries rotting and whiteflies dancing.

I found a ball of hair,
a needle, a string worm
wrapped around his guts.

I sucked through the horn
and filled my mouth
with   pus.

Inside his belly
I heard the winds belch.
Chanting that
eating his heart
was the curse of his eye.

Picking Leftovers

There's men in the cellar shovelling, sweeping with combs and tooth-brushes, probing dental picks, doctors in surgical gloves cradling bones, jaws, teeth, skulls, brittle arms and legs. Glueing pieces through lenses thicker than god's eye, given birth dates and pencilled in bibles.

When I was a child, father would stop at sites we called picking leftovers. I've returned with pitchfork in my hand, hammer against my heart. I've offered tobacco to earth and raked layers of toilet bowls, tin cans, beer bottles, and open-mouthed refrigerators. The skin of earth peels leaking pails, stench buried in ceremony. And over there in marble fields boxes of bones cemented in white rock. I give them birth dates, carefully record locations and fax the findings to the ship docked, waiting for hundreds of years, on the eastern shore.

Diaper Boy

I was a kid my diapers full,
my legs chapped, lying against the slop pail.
They found me mosquito-bitten, snot all over
my face, flies dancing free.

I was a naked starving mouse.

I was alone in the log shack,
my mother and father at the
beer parlour. Somebody walked by and heard
my cry.

•

See my long black, black braids?
I grease them with bear fat and gloss them.
Put on my stetson,
tie a red bandana around my neck,
charm the women with beer and cigarettes.
Fill them with babies.

I make women hold me.

They can't resist
my hard dark body.
I move like a mounting deer.
They caress and stroke the same arms that froze
beside that slop pail.

They kiss the snot off my face where the flies
no longer dance.

•

My ears only hear the soft warm panting.

Jahnnie

Jahnnie used to stand on the gravel
at the edge of the reserve,
his arm extended, thumb pointing up,
a burlap sack slung over his shoulder.

Eight o'clock in the morning,
driving by in my jalopy,
still rubbing the sleep from my eyes,
the radio rooster blasting the air.
I'd stop, pick Jahnnie up.

He'd open the rusty hinged door,
crawl in with a smile and ask,
"Huz's da g-earls?"
Stale cigarette smoke and home-brewed beer
would sting my eyes.

His brylcreamed hair smelled of greasy neckbones,
his face oily from mouth to cheek.
He'd fumble in his burlap sack,
clanking cans and spilling aged beer
from ditch-gathered bottles.

"Ciganet?" he'd ask.

Each summer each day I'd pick Jahnnie up,
his dirty blue jeans,
the silver of his hair,
stoop of his back.

The yellow stain of his beer
sank in the sofa of my jalopy seat.

His toothless old mouth,
caved-in cheeks,
sagging shallow pools
beneath his eyes,
dragging his burlap sack
smoking his "ciganet."
I'd watch him straggle
his beloved gravel road,
a spiritless coyote.

Lonesome Charlie,
whiskey and beer
"ciganets and da g-earls"
had their ride in my Pontiac
and Jahnnie's skeleton's back.

Idylwyld Crow

Rushing home
into the dark
I drive by
a moving scarecrow.

Red cap
perched on
grey corn-husk hair,
toothless mouth
jutting jaw.

Can't help but stop
and offer her a ride.
In broken English
she tells me she lives in
Kilburn.

Pulls out her blue
hospital card with
her address
explaining all the while

she's been out
buying the cheapest
stale bread in town
somewhere on Idylwyld.

A Saulteaux,
a dark crow,
feeding her children
crumbs in the city light.

Sister

In the morgue *ê-pimisihk*
on a steel table.

Scarred face
crushed.
Work boots
trampled her in.

Her arm crooked,
limp by her side,
vagina raw, bleeding,
stuffed with a beer bottle.

pasikôk, pasikôk
pêhtawihk, pêhtawihk
kisîmisinaw pîkiskwêw

âhkosiwak ayisiyiniwak
piko matotisânihk ta-pimâtisiyahk
kiyipa, kîwêk

Race with your spirits
kâkîsimotâk, to heal, to heal.

iskwêw atoskêwin kimiyikonaw.
kakwêyâhok, kakwêyâhok.

pasikôk, pasikôk
pêhtawihk, pêhtawihk
kisîmisinaw pîkiskwêw.

âhkosiwak ayisiyiniwak
piko matotisânihk ta-pimâtisiyahk
kiyipa, kîwêk.
Race with your spirits
ta-kâkîsimoyahk, to heal, to heal
iskwêw atoskêwin kimiyikonaw
kakwêyâhok, kakwêyâhok
ahâw.

Beneath the Eyelids

She crossed the barrier of the mind
just before sleep slid over the eyelids
and *pâhkahkos* flooded the thin skin.

Blood ran down the skull face,
strands of black hair in patches.
Her jaw hung loose, crooked to one side.

She wailed.
The cry spun
beneath the armpit of the trees,

floated like thick smoke
to sit on the mountain tops.
Her weight was heavy on the backs of the people.

They scrambled below her, trying
to pray, to sing.
Still the bombs fell and the black grease spread.

pâhkahkos, with her emptiness, sits
heavy with death
waning slowly as each moon
slips
beneath her eyelids.

Eclipse

As the earth travelled
between the sun
and the moon
I was a dog tearing flesh
inside my skin.
I paced the hall
swinging my head,
the rabid blood
flooding my eyes.
The moon slipped
through the sheet of dark.
I too waned
and the rainberry
words sprung from my
fingers.

so sorry

the pope said i'm sorry
i sent a useless sack of scalped
potatoes.

he said indian agents would
give Daddy a roll of twine,
a box of shells and whisky.
the spirits crawled inside
my daddy and never left.

he sent blankets
and my babies died.
he sent wooden sticks
with a dead man to hang
around my neck.

he said if i prayed
to you, geezuz,
ate your body, drank
your blood,
threw out my bannock,
lived on my knees
counting stones,

i'd never be without
my family.

I'm So Sorry

i'm so sorry, the pope said
i thought you were just gathering
to lift your legs, thump your chest
around that tree of old men.
i didn't know the rock and twig
you smoked,
blueberries, and Sweetgrass
were your offerings.
i wouldn't have taken your babies
and fed them wafers and wine.

i'm so sorry, i just thought
we could borrow land for a little
to plant our seeds,
raise sheep and build churches, schools.
i really didn't know how you survived
for centuries on Buffalo and teepees,
praying in Medicine Wheels.

i'm so sorry, i should have told
the settlers to quit their scalping.
selling hair at two bits for each Indian
i'm so sorry. i'm so sorry.
maybe i could build healing churches,
chapels full of Sweetgrass and Drums,
chase the Spirits out and fill Sweatlodges
full of armed angels.

ten hail marys

the pope said too bad that
man of sea, kelp, rancid pig,
and starving teeth
came on your land.

i'm awfully sorry he ate so
much buffalo meat
gave you beads and trinkets
for beaver, coyote, and mink.

he didn't mean to sleep with
your women, make them cry
and send your children to
purgatory and england too.

i'm sorry the pope said.
i'll write to the priest, the nuns,
make them say, i'm sorry too
for *suffering little children*
coming to me in the red brick
schools.

i'll tell other people too
i'm sorry and i promise to
fold my hands and keep you
in my prayers.

In Da Name of Da Fadder

In da name of da fadder, poop
on my knees I pray to geezuz
cuz I got mad at my husband for
humpin' and makin too many babies
I 'pologize cuz I mad and cried I
didn't have no bannock and lard
to feed dem cuz my husband
drank all da *sôniyâs* for wine.

In da name of da fadder, poop
my husband slap, fist and kick me
I hit him back. I 'pologize poop
da priest said I must of done someding
wrong and I deserve it cuz woman is
'uppose to listen to man. I not a good
wife cuz my hands somedimes
want to kill him.

In da name of da fadder, poop
I lookit other man he is so
handsome my eyes hurt, he kind, gentle,
soft laugh and my body wants to
feel his hot face. I no geezuz
would be mad he said I must not
be durty in my doughts but
poop I want smile and warm arms.

In da name of da fadder, poop
inside the sweatlodge I shame cuz
Indian *iskwêw* don't no anydin',
in church priest said all us pagans
will go to hell. I don't no what dat means,
all I no I is big sinner
and maybe I won't see geezuz when I die.

In da name of da fadder, poop
I dought da geezuz kind but
I is no good. I can't read hen write.
I don't understand how come *môniyâs* has
clean howse and lottsa feed and he don't
share it with me and my children.
I don't understand why geezuz say I be
poor, stay on welfare cuz *môniyâs* say
I good for nuddin' cuz I don't have
wisdom. Forgive me poop I is
big sinner.

der poop

der poop
forgive me for writing on dis newspaper
I found it in da outhouse, saw lines
dat said you is sorry
some of my Indian friends say is good but
some of dem say you sorry don't walk
so I was sitting here dinking dat we
maybe dalk
say, I always want to dell you stay
out of my pissness
if me wants to dalk to drees
and build nests in hawse
dats hup to me
if me wants to pitch my dent
and feed da ghost bannock hen berries
and maybe drow some Indian popcorn
for you geezuz dats hup to me
I don't hask forgiveness not want
hand marys, or a step ladder to heaven
me is happy with da sky, da bird *iyiniwak*,
four-legged *iyiniwak*, I is happy
sorry mean dat I don't need yous church
and yous priest delling me what to do
sorry mean dat I free to dalk to *manitow*
the spirits and plant *iyiniwak.*
dats all for now, poop
maybe we dalk again next dime I see you
in da newspaper.

my ledders

der poop
I no, I no, you dired of my ledders
I couldn't let dis one go
I dought you could do somedin 'bout it.
years ago you stopped *nôhkom* and *nimosôm*
from praying in da sweatlodge and sundance,
drummin, singin and dancin.
you even stopped dem from Indian speakin
and storydellin.
well you must had some kind of bower
cuz da govment sure listen.

well, poop
last night on DV
I watched some whitemen
sweat in da lodge, and at
dinner dime on da radio
I heard dat man dell us
dat some darafist was havin a retreat
and to register.
what dat mean, I not sure.
anyway he is buildin' a sweatlodge.
I never hear anybody before on da radio
dell da whole world dat.
I sure suprise and kinda make me mad.

I wonder if you could dell da govment
to make dem laws dat stop dat
whiteman from dakin our *isistâwina*
cuz I dell you poop
i don't dink you like it
if I dook you
gold cup and wine
pass it 'round our circles
cuz I don't have you drainin
from doze schools.
I haven't married you geezuz
and I don't kneel to him,
cuz he ain't my god.

dese men, poop, don't know what
tobacco mean, what suffer mean,
alls dey no is you geezuz die for dem
dey don't no what fastin' mean
dey jist dake and gobble our *matotisân*
as if dey own it.
dey don't no what it mean to dake
from da earth and give somedin' back
I so dired of all dis *kimotiwin,* poop
deach your children.
eat your geezuz body.
drink his blood.
dell dem to go back to dere own deachings,
poop.

Returning

It's raining, and the salt slides down my face into my mouth. Blue Quills Residential School, the log cabin. Memories. I summon them all.

I have been asked many times, wasn't residential school better than the fires that raged at home? I don't find that a fair question. My grasshopper legs clung only to the crippled love I came to know. It lay for years snared within the red walls of the residential school. Such shame. Such assault. That's what it was, refined under the rule of reading, writing, and arithmetic, and a god that had the eyes of a roving fly. This god wore black robes, cowls, and beads. Pebble beads, hard and polished as wind-swept rocks with silver and wood crosses where jesus died for my sins.

I grew up behind those walls. Six years. I knelt each morning in the chapel, up at dawn to pray to jesus to save my soul. I hoped that I would win an award for being the most pious, most committed at the end of the year. I can't help it when the buds between my legs tingle. I can't help it when my eyes stray to explore the tits of other girls. Why must I hide my body, jesus? The rags that I wear when I shower are so heavy, will I ever be clean? The scrub brush is not hard enough.

And jesus, can you tell me how to love a boy? I must not have such dirty thoughts or I will get purgatory and venial sin. I can't tell the priest in the confessional, so I write my sins and ask for penance.

At night I leave tears. I want my mother, my father, my brothers, my sister. I hold a sucker from my brother underneath my pillow. For weeks I take only a lick. I peek at my brothers across the dining room. I mustn't look too long. Why can't I look and talk to my brothers? At home during the laughing bloom of leaves we fight and cheat at our games. They call me ugly and flat chested. I hate them. In them I see my father, double tongues of laughter spinning my thoughts. Yet we work together and marvel at the wood stacked for our parents. We want to surprise them, but they never say a word. They too are the children of residential school. We know only how to show anger. We are always suspicious of one another. Watching, forever watching.

The little girls hate me. There is one with big lips assigned to the ruler. I hate her. She slaps us hard. We stand around the girl with white skin when it's her turn to have her hair combed. One, two, three, ah, the numbers are too great. Lice. We are in awe, yet we shame her as she wins the count. At home my mother creams my hair with kerosene and I sit till all the bugs are dead. With gentle hands she pulls white nits. I listen to her murmur stories of *wîsahkêcâhk*. Her hands are two dead branches at her side when I leave for residential school. I see her next, when the pussy willows green. Her eyes will be bruised and black.

Father hands me the butcher knife and tells me to take over the skinning of the deer, but first he salts the fresh kidneys he's brought home. He never tells me, but I hear him brag that I'm a good little skinner. I never know when the thunder will burst, never know when the lightning will strike. My memories roll inside my stomach. Mean little butterflies at home, and at residential school.

The supervisor has huge keys hanging from her skirt. Everywhere we go she pulls her keys to unlock the stores of toilet paper, towels, Sunday morning tams. We are given three sheets of toilet paper. We learn to fold and refold. A hundred little squares of shit squeezed inside my heart. I didn't know I had locked away these memories, the keys jingling in the corridor of other people's stories.

I remember my first kiss. I received it on the staircase, treasured the feel of my first love's mouth for months. I didn't know what to do with him. Love was saliva, tongues of tobacco smoke, the hidden spirits.

Yet, when the life in my belly kicked and milk trickled down my breasts the mountains called. The sweet sweetgrass smoke and the sweatlodge rocks woke my spirit. I knew then where I was cradled.

You've Got to Teach White Women Everything

I've tasted myself.
Gooseberries, pin cherries and
rosehips rolled between my teeth,
stretched till my bones bent
and my breath was wind.

I've tasted the tongue of
bear, deer and dog,
left camomile in the corners of my
mouth.

I've tasted
the sweet drip of sea
drying between my thighs,
belly sweat breathing
on my breast.

I've tasted chocolate raisins
on my spine, rolling raspberries
between my toes and the breath
of swallows, feathers on my face.

I've tasted
till I'm swollen with sleep.

These Are the Body's Gifts

I offer ribs, taut flesh stretched like a starving dog's. My
tits scratching sidewalks.

I offer belly, wedged in spandex. A pit of balled snakes
quivering beneath touch.

I offer buttocks, rump of deer sailing over fences.
wêpâyôs: white tail flipping.

I offer thighs, the smoke of a .303, fingers unclenched.

Take this body of snails and leeches. Stretched babies that
have left dried creek beds across the gut.

Take it, take it, pressed tight in your beak.
Beady eyes examining its old, tender flaws.
Marvel at the rot.

Inside you, Magpie, I will be the glutton eating flesh,
curing the dysentery of age.

For Usine

A pigeon gathers pebbles on the freeway
sidestepping the traffic.
A ladybug walks on the edge of a large envelope
on my husband's desk.
The death of a tree goes unnoticed,
a deep white glare rooted to the earth.
My son's girlfriend leaves robot kisses on the telephone.

I've squirted my baby boy in the eyes
with my left breast, suckled him with both.
His teeth chewed the teats like rubber.

The black fur of a flattened dog outlined
on the pavement.
There is no game, no fur, no berries
just bones and chains at Mendel Art Gallery.
Laughter of nursery children under the glass
teepee at *wânaskêwin*.

My breasts are kneaded buckskin, his baby fingers
grooved into the smooth folds of skin.
We saved his penis from the slicing knife.

At thirteen my sister wiped the smells,
filling my diaper with fresh moss.
She stopped my wails with her large toe,
unable to find the soother filled with cow milk.

In grade one he clung, screaming. My stretched breast
empty. He slept with a wooden sword. At dawn he laughed
at a battle he'd won with a skeleton of clothes.

We were hungry. My brother and I squeezed the
infant rabbits from twisted guts. Dug small
potatoes, wild onions and made a broth. Wrapped
bannock dough on willow. Sugarbeet parents never knew.

He was standing on a float with a chainsaw larger than
the baby skunk he cradled. Threw candies at his
sister and me. I grinned, yelled through the crowd, I love
you, my baby. Years later I learned how the snare of pride
and shame strung him.

The wind tears leaves off sleeping trees. The magpies
are cocky. Soon they'll be black specks against frozen
white. I hope I can keep the car on the road. My hands are
my eyes guiding the steering wheel over black matted fur. My
hands caress the curves of my breast and hibernate with the
ladybug, hopscotch between hundreds of rolling
tires, send puckered kisses to bald-headed babies. They are
bark of dead trees. My hands limp while my baby answers
Janice's call, puckering the air.

I dream a ghost speaking through my body. Three nights of
dreaming. I drink four cups of coffee, my eye bags reaching
the brim. I don't sleep till I hear his footsteps above
my bed.

His first girlfriend was a short fat kid. She was twelve
with long tousled hair. She acted like a starved-loved cat,
rubbing up and down his leg.

My cousin said she was three when the dirty old man first
touched her. Her memories are dead inside her, when the
little snake crawls between her legs they are alive. I
remember peeing in the dark outside the beer parlour,
that dirty old man was suppose to keep an eye out. I ran and
ran with my panties down.

Me, I'll keep my snot, fold my squares of kleenex.

I hope he wears rubbers.

For Omeasoo

I lift my wrist
suck out marrow
blow into my daughter.
I spoon the spill
into her lips.

I lift my mother's finger,
add *nôhkom's* ashes,
and stir.

My daughter dances
a leaf twirling
on the wind.

She blows the baritone
a gosling calling,
kîwêtinohk.
She delivers
dried meat and croissants
to *nôhkomak*.

She is a rainbow,
the give-away feast
of our blood.
She bleeds.

For Patrick

I held him on the hill
water on his face
the bruised scales glistened on his back
beneath the full moon.
He cupped his hands
offered his soul. I took,
filled his body with trees;
he hacked and sawed for spare change.
Filled his body with women and children;
he danced them with whisky and longings
of the hills, turned and walked his road,
kicking gravel in his way.
Always his pipe tobacco lingered.

I filled his eyes with cheating men
rolling in fat thighs,
gambling cowboys on the tracks.
A magpie stealing guts in skidrow,
vomiting them in his maggot nest.
Silver coins in his eyes,
window pane on his tongue,
soaring through glass and shrapnel,
his childhood left
on the hill of his back.

I filled his mouth with skunk juice,
rat-root and honey. I clipped his wings, one flew
to an Indian woman who wove it into blankets.
His teeth sit on a pelt by his bed.

His memories blood skies, his father's bullet,
the leather whip of his hand,
his beak attacking stories of the heart.
From the earth he draws my breath,
music of frogs, crickets, cats and dogs,
wolves and bears.
And a woman.
Always the tobacco lingers.

Landscape

I have set his feet on soft ground;
I have set his feet on the sloping shoulders of the world.
— Sheila Watson

I've walked the land till ravines swallowed my feet.

Tobacco was offered to fire and earth
the fire came out to lick the dead grass. That spring
the cabin burned where I had filled my life with laughter
and anger. Only the cellar is left.

A young girl, a two-year-old boy cry with coyotes,
their mother's bones mending in the hospital,
their father selling horses and cattle for wine.
I see them running along the creek, two young coyotes
yelping. I take the .22 and fire into the air.

Many winters have passed and the coyotes have grown straggly
with hunger, their eyes shrivelled rosehips.
Their yelping has turned into moans. Years ago
wîhtikow reached inside their guts, where its roots grew
into their hair, into their fingers and feet, their hearts
frozen. Coyote pups now roam that creek, sniffing
for their parents. They run side by side, hungry.

I dreamt I was filling the cracks of the cabin
with paper and books while the wind told stories. An old
bear lit the coal oil lamp. In her hand she held sweetgrass.
Later climbing a hill I found four feathers, and
three coyotes following.

I've become arched feet inside my shoes. I will find those
.22 bullets and hit the mark.

The Way to the Heart

wîhtikow travels
with a hatchet, bladder pail
and snares.
His ragged moccasin feet bare
to thistles, to rocks, to snow.

He boils robins and sparrows.
The tiny bones stain
necklaces, little skulls on breasts.
He lives a lonely life
filled with relatives in his gut,
dreaming of fat Indians
in the deep of winter.

wîhtikow and *wîsahkêcâhk* meet.
wîsahkêcâhk is a laughing fox,
coyote, and word-hustler.
Chickadee sings about the time *wîsahkêcâhk*
ate dry meat-scabs that fell off his rump.

wîhtikow casts a spell.
He thinks.

wîsahkêcâhk dances,
building fires for *wîhtikow*. Dancing the feast of death.
sihkos, slender weasel, little brother
pokes his breath
to watch the dance and feast of bones.
Dance, oh dance, little brother,

travel the back hole of
wîhtikow. Cut the straps
inside his chest. Tomorrow
you will be most celebrated.

And when *wîhtikow* blew
the fire rose, the back hole
opened, foul wind breathed.
Little brother travelled
up the dark passage
to the North
and the heart of *wîhtikow* was cut.

wîsahkêcâhk, spirit of vision
wîhtikow, spirit of twisted hunger,
they dance, they dance,
come alive, come alive. Let
tobacco speak, the spirit
of *sihkos* will free you.

The Heat of My Grandmothers

The old man calls my *nôhkomak*
a bunch of bitches, *pisikwâtisiw*.

Yes, I took painted warriors:
molded their sinew thighs,
into my flesh.
Our spirits moaned, laughing between
teepee poles reaching the heavens,
stars leaping against the breathing hide.

I was fourteen winters when I was told
my first husband was the elder's choice.
That winter in our teepee
the smoke couldn't hide
the fragrance
of muskeg tea
and juniper
we mixed between our bodies.
The second winter two calves
dropped to the earth.

My first husband's bones
I found beneath the autumn buffalo,
his arrows in the meat. My moccasins heavy,
I swayed the roundness of my body
wailed till the buffalo sweat
melted his skin into
the prairie grass.

My second husband of three winters
I received at a give-away between
the Blackfoot and Cree. He kissed
the valleys of my buttocks, licked
the paths of my swollen breast. He,
antelope of clouds. I,
wider than his open mouth.

I found him after a skirmish with
the white meat, a bullet between his eyes.
I was winter in my spring. My braids
greyer than the passing snow. I called
magpie, crow, and raven to clean
his body cradled in the trees.

My third husband took my calves and
gave them to the black robes. His
eyes bluer than mountain rivers, hands
took half the hide I made for travois. He'd
flicker his eyelashes; monarchs in my sleep,
while I dreamt of babies hungry and
frightened behind cold fences.

Ten babies. Six of prairie blood, four
of meeting rivers. A beaded rainbow,
each child suckled by my wind-bitten nipples
their fathers loved.

Roots and Wings

In the brief exchange
both dog and woman
knew he was willed
beneath the fender and the wheels.
Their eyes
met before he left.

He wasn't the first dog
to go.
Her mind twisted their guts
hands laying their skulls
under saplings.
There will be no dogs
in the city.

In dance
the Spirits lifted her,
she pinched her arms as she watched
herself float.
The squirrels talked about virgins
and newlyweds.
The water wanted to know
where she would go.

Her husband was the healer.
He went in the sweatlodge,
ate the people's offering
of deer and rabbit roast.
He was given Eagle feathers

while she
received the thousand eyes of flies.

The cats arched, scratched and hissed
behind the half-ton cab.
She knew
she'd find their fingernails
in a ball of bones and fur,
the owl's feast of fat.

In the woods with ink and paper leaves
she met her lover. He flowing beneath
her feet, crackling knuckles in the wind,
gurgling near the beaver dam. They argued
about geezuz and the origin of man, spun stories
in the dance of their tongues.

•

Her husband said he was reaching
forty and wished to plant roots.
In sleep she visited fields
of wheat and straw,
dancing in waves, wrapped in
clouds. The trees cradled her,
passing her
back and forth,
arm to arm.

The city never sees the dawn.
A magpie scolds her return.
The water's tongue is frozen beneath
hot sewage and glacial barges.
She keeps falling down carpet stairs.
The Spirits laugh in darkness
while the silence eats.

The fruitful feast of forty:
cranberries and currants,
hives in high branches,
thorns catching jeans, scratches
of bears at anthills, calling
loons in blueberry flats,
all caught on paper leaves.
She's flown with the best of them,
free in their knowing.

The dogs are in the city
tonguing rain off her face.
Their guts wring
in her fingers, skulls howling
in the trees, moon lovers in
meadows.

The woods map her dreams,
the west wind braids
strands of grey hair
to the earth in her feet.

The Eagle Squeeze

I've wandered the wilderness
running after your shadow
plucking fluffs from your belly
dragging my cord.
The eggs in your mouth
you dropped at my doorstep,
babies featherless as your smile.

I'm skinned-drum,
beating stick in your hand.
My tits flat.
I throb thick,
old bloody stories sung.
Rat-root trickling
through my heart. Steam from your body
sweating into my robes,
bones buckling beneath the rock.

        Yes, I snuggle deep into him,
        twenty years of wind he blows in his sleep.
        Yes, I've swum and swallowed
        the slippery sweat of his pores.
        My belly drummed
        little heels against my heart.
        I've cried, cursed, and laughed the
        raw babies.
        Yes, we ate off boxes,
        selling his grandfather's coins for food.
        Built our first table with planks

the Spirits lifted.
He Sundanced,
the dew on my cheeks won't rub away.

Your thunder drums
on my waiting belly.
Your wings span the prairie warriors dance.
Dip and bend,
    dip and bend,
dip and bend
feather fluffs,
clouds and tents open in the sun.
My outstretched palm heavy, gold
reflecting in your eye.

Yes, many hours I spend alone,
children hanging from my tits.
He slumbered over formaldehyde
pickled bodies of the dead.
Yes, I touched the warm space beside my bed,
he rushing out in forty below
to patch the beaten drunk,
hold the widow,
and deliver the frozen baby.
Yes, frogs mat the carpet
beneath my feet
and I wear the Onassis dress.
We are spoons in sleep,
butterflies fluttering on my neck,
sweet whisperings, sweetgrass in the air.

The shadow dances
hanging from my neck.
I move from the rock
gathering goose eggs.
I shall weave my basket
from the hairs I pluck from
your brown arms,
spin my lover's eyes, emerald suns.
I shall fill my belly
with the spill from your beak.
I'll fold the eggs
in winter skin
cradled in sleep.
My grandmother's rump
hot and broad as your prairie wings.

GLOSSARY

ahcahk . . . . soul, spirit

apisc-âhkiskôs . . . . large prairie chicken

asam . . . . feed

awâsisak . . . . children

ayamihâwina . . . . rituals, prayer

ayisiyiniw . . . . human being, person

âmow-mêyi . . . . honey (literal translation: bee shit)

âstam . . . . come

câhcâmosikan . . . . sneezing root

ê-pimisihk . . . . she lays

hâw . . . . now, okay

isistâwina . . . . rituals

iskwêw . . . . woman

iyiniwak . . . . People

kimotiwin . . . . theft, stealing

kinêpik . . . . snake

kiskiman . . . . sharp tail bone (literal translation: file)

kîmôc . . . . in secret

kîwêtinohk . . . . north, going home

manitow . . . . Creator, God

matotisân . . . . sweatlodge

micakisîs . . . . little gut, penis

mihkwâskikan . . . . robin (literal translation: red-breast)

môniyâs . . . . white person

namôya mâskôc . . . . probably not

nêhiyawak . . . . the Cree, the People

nimosôm . . . . my grandfather

nitôtêm . . . . my friend; my kinsman

nîcimos . . . . girlfriend, boyfriend

nôhkom . . . . my grandmother

nôhkom âtayôhkân . . . . Grandmother of the legends

nôhkomak . . . . my grandmothers

paskwâw-mostos . . . . buffalo

pâhkahkos . . . . Flying Skeleton, mythical spirit
of the Cree

pê-kîwê . . . . come home

picikîskisîs . . . . chickadee

pisikwâtisiw . . . . loose, run around

sihkos . . . . weasel

sôniyâs . . . . money

wânaskêwin . . . . tranquility, to make a turn in life,
a heritage site in Saskatoon

wêpâyôs . . . . wagging tail

wîhtikow . . . . Ice being, cannibal

wîsahkêcâhk . . . . Cree trickster

Stanza from page 58
(This song is sung by many Plains Cree people.)

waniskâ . . . . Arise

pê-wâpan ôma . . . . dawn arrives

âsay piyêsîsak . . . . already birds

nikamowak . . . . sing

miyohtâkwan . . . . it sounds beautiful

kitaskînaw . . . . our earth, our land

Stanza from pages 107 and 108

pasikôk, pasikôk . . . . Get up, get up

pêhtawihk, pêhtawihk . . . . . listen, listen (as in: hear, hear)

kisîmisinaw pîkiskwêw . . . . . our younger sibling speaks

âhkosiwak ayisiyiniwak . . . . the people are sick

piko matotisânihk

   ta-pimâtisiyahk . . . . we must go into the sweatlodge
                                to be alive

kiyipa, kîwêk . . . . hurry, go home

kakîsimotâk . . . . let's pray, implore

iskwêw atoskêwin

   kimiyikonaw . . . . a woman delegated work to us

kakwêyâhok,

   kakwêyâhok . . . . hurry, hurry

ta-kâkîsimoyahk . . . . let's all pray

ahâw . . . . it's okay, amen

AFTERWORD —
COMFORTABLE IN MY BONES

In the Northern woods of Saskatchewan lies a creek; in the summer, it's a slender, lazy snail. When the spring rains come, it becomes a writhing snake creating turbulent waves, carrying everything before it. I walked the woods, following the creek, cradling paper leaves and talking stick, tobacco and sweetgrass in my hands. On many occasions, I flew over logs in front of me eager to gain my solitude, eager to unload the discoveries I held close to my heart. My favourite spot overlooked the banks where I leaned against an old log I shared with ants. There, I contemplated something I had read, something I heard on CBC, something I dreamt, a conversation I had with my children or my husband. Sometimes, these discoveries were not pretty. My journeys became a ritual where I offered tobacco and smudged with sweetgrass. Whatever travelled into my thoughts, I immediately wrote, no matter how absurd or obscure. At times, I did nothing but breathe, listen and sleep, comfortable in my bones. The landscape of the earth and my mind were both simple and complex. I bore feelings that needed song. I often suffered the rash of shame bursting through the thin layers of skin. Yet my spirit demanded the spring of clear blood. I saw no need to run. The land, the Spirit doesn't betray you. I was learning to cry with the Spirit. I was safe to tear, to lick, to strip the stories from my bones and to offer them to the universe.

When I was a child, I was taught to lift a found bone from the earth and scrape my warts, then to return it the way it was found. Many times, I watched my cousin grind bones for my grandmother, medicines she added to her bundles. I was grinding my own bones. Through the leaves and pen, the elusive became concrete. My voice rose through my scribble. On many occasions, I had watched my grandfather's long johns held by a string, flopping, waving, rolling on the edge of the culvert. We always knew when laundry day was. The foam the creek made provided the soap he didn't have. During our courting days, my husband and I would strip in the spring April heat, bask in the sun and plunge in the glacial Whiterabbit River on Kootenay Plains. The strength of the water replenishes and destroys, the calling of the creek and my return are a natural process.

The year rolled into two, three, four: my journals accumulated. The Great Mystery entered my dreams, and I heard its voice through its creation. Squirrels shared their chatter, the wind blew its soul into my ears, and the water spoke its very ancient tongue. These stirrings were not unfamiliar since I come from a place where all creation and its gifts are naturally accepted. I went to the elders and spoke to them about my dreams and my revelations. I entered ritual once again to receive my spiritual name and honour my journey. I had a dream many years ago that I was repairing the cabin I grew up in with paper and books. I had entered this ceremony, the stirring of my marrow, a living prayer of building and healing, feeding my soul. I read a wide range of authors, including Joseph Campbell, Carl Jung, Mary Daly, Matthew Fox, Sheila Watson, Louise Erdrich, and numerous anthologies written by female and Native writers. My curiosity challenged, I covered topics around sexual morals, philosophy, religious and spiritual debates, symbols, myths and legends. I hoarded my solitude jealously, and became angry when I wasn't fulfilling these needs.

The map of oral storytelling had long been laid out for me. I often entertained my children with legends I grew up with or made up on my own through the images in classical music. Writing was a natural process. The stories inside me demanded face. They became my medicine, creating themselves in the form of poetry. These egg-bones were the voice which I have been addressing. My bare feet had felt the drum of the earth and the heartbeat of my palms. I did not fight these stories, though many times I wanted to run. I became a wolf, sniffing and searching, pawing, muzzling, examining every visible track I made or saw. I became the predator on the scent. I was the master, the slave, beholder and beheld, the voice and the song. I was the dark, the light. Like the legend of *pâhkahkos*, my death-song grated, and when I honoured my history *pâhkahkos* rattled her bones in the gourds of my memory. I will no longer be a binding sinew of stifling rules, but rather a sinew of wolf songs, clear as morning air.

Louise B. Halfe – Sky Dancer
1994

ACKNOWLEDGMENTS

I am deeply indebted to the Great Mystery, the Great Parent of All, to the Dream Guardians (*pawâkanak*), to the Memory of my grandparents and my parents, and to the Saddle Lake Community. Thank you to Brick Books and their staff for believing in the continuous life of *Bear Bones & Feathers*. Finally, to Jean Okimâsis and Arok Wolvengrey and who bravely provided the Cree nuances and spelling. All of my relations.

mistahi ninanâskomâwak kisê-manitow — mâmawi-ohtâwîmâw — êkwa mîna pawâkanak; nimiyo-kiskisitotawâwak nôhkomak, nimosômak êkwa ninîkihikwak êkwa kahkiyaw aniki onihcikiskwapiwinihk kâ-ohcîcik. nitatamihikwak aniki kâ-atoskêcik *Brick Brooks* ê-âhkami-tâpwêwakêyihtahkik '**maskokana êkwa mîkwanak**' (*Bear Bones & Feathers*). iskwêyâc, ninanâskomâwak *Jean Okimâsis* êkwa *Arok Wolvengrey* iyikohk kâ-sôhkêyimocik ta-wîcihicik kwayask nêhiyaw-itwêwina ta-itwêmakahki êkwa ta-itasinahamihk. kahkiyaw niwâhkômâkanitik.

Louise Bernice Halfe – Sky Dancer was raised on Saddle Lake Reserve and attended Blue Quills Residential School. Her first book, *Bear Bones & Feathers*, received the 1996 Milton Acorn People's Poetry Award and was a finalist for the Spirit of Saskatchewan Award, the Pat Lowther Award, and the Gerald Lampert Award. *Blue Marrow* was a finalist for the 1998 Governor General's Award for Poetry. *The Crooked Good* won the First Peoples' Publishing Award and the Saskatoon Book Award in 2008 and was short-listed for the Pat Lowther Award. Her fourth book, *Burning in This Midnight Dream,* won the 2017 Saskatchewan Book Award and the Raymond Souster Award, among numerous other awards. In 2018, as part of the Laurier Poetry Series, her previously published works were compiled in *Sôhkêyihta: The Poetry of Sky Dancer Louise Bernice Halfe* (edited by David Gaertner). Halfe was Saskatchewan's Poet Laureate for 2005–2006, was awarded the

Latner Writers Trust Award for her body of work in 2017, and was awarded the 2020 Kloppenburg Award for Literary Excellence. She trained at Nechi Institute as a facilitator, has a Bachelor of Social Work, was granted a lifetime membership in the League of Canadian Poets, and has received three honorary doctorates. In January of 2021, Louise was selected to be Canada's 9th Parliamentary Poet Laureate, serving until December 2022. She currently works with Elders in the organization Opikinawasowin ("raising our children") and lives on the Prairies with her husband, Peter.